£149

DH

To Diana
with Love from the Children

RIGHT: *I hope you can dance
with the angels.
Love Phoebe x   Age 6*

Photographs by Ruth Corney
Text by Robert Spencer

PICCADILLY PRESS · LONDON

I would like to thank the following people for their help and advice:

Deborah Smith for her design skills, all the technical and reception staff at Joe's Basement, Euston, Julie Taylor, Clive and Paul Gringras, Elly Van der Hoorn, Tanya Laurel, Phoebe and Fraser. Thank you to my family for their encouragement and enthusiasm. I am indebted to Mark and Joe for their love and to Abu for being there. Thanks also to all at Piccadilly Press.

Ruth Corney

Text copyright © George Robert Maurice Spencer, 1998
Children's tributes, photographs copyright © Ruth Corney, 1998
Photographs of Diana copyright © P A News

Designed by Judith Robertson
Cover photographs by John Stillwell copyright © P A News, 1996, 1997
Cover design by Lucille Chomowicz

Printed and bound in Belgium by Proost
for the publishers Piccadilly Press Ltd., 5 Castle Road, London NW1 8PR

A catalogue record for this book is available from the British Library

ISBN: 1 85340 424 1

The publisher gratefully acknowledges the permission of the children to reproduce their letters. The publisher has not been able to identify a number of the authors whose letters have been published. The publisher invites those children to write in and claim a complimentary copy of this book.

Introduction

I was driving home, after dining out with friends, when I heard that Diana had been taken to hospital following an accident. While I was preparing for bed, I heard the shattering news that she was dead. I was stunned. My telephone soon started ringing with friends and family, and I shared with Diana's sister, Jane, our feelings of horror and disbelief. I flew back to London just as soon as I could.

The outpouring of grief from the nation really surprised me. I viewed the tributes at Kensington Palace, Buckingham Palace and Westminster Abbey and was overwhelmed by the atmosphere. Thousands of people talking softly showed much respect and sadness.

At the time I only had a chance to read snippets from these tributes. Looking at the outstanding photographs in this book and studying the sentiments expressed by the children, I am even more impressed by the strength of feeling and the love displayed by these young people. It is appropriate that we are recording some of these tributes for posterity.

Robert Spencer

April, 1998

Diana
As a PRINCESS

*C*hildren throughout the world admired the way Diana looked in the lovely gowns and sparkling jewels. She embodied their view of what a fairy princess should be.

As Princess of Wales she was friendly with heads of state, chief ministers and rulers in this country and overseas. Diana travelled widely while working for Britain; she developed her role as an ambassador in such an exciting way. Despite the demands of her job and of being watched by so many people, Diana retained her delightful sense of humour, and encouraged those with her to relax and enjoy the activities in which she was involved. She undertook her duties avoiding any sense of pomposity.

RIGHT: *To Diana,
Queen of Hearts.
Love Alfred Mizen school*

LEFT: *Our Queen of Hearts, Diana,*
You were so special to everyone.
May you rest in peace.
All my love, Adele   Age 10

RIGHT: *Diana, our princess,*
We didn't know we loved you
until you were gone.
Love from Annette, Eddie and Eva   Age 3

Diana
As a BEAUTY

Diana was attractive as a young girl. Probably she was a bit lonely, awkward and insecure as her sisters were four and six years older than she was and her parents were divorced. This may have been why she didn't appreciate her looks and took so many years to conquer her shyness.

After Diana married, the family expected much interest, but it was a surprise that 'Di-mania' so captured the imagination of the people and the press.

Children everywhere saw Diana as a rare beauty with striking features. Whatever she wore she looked lovely; she retained her special princess quality even in an exercise outfit.

LEFT: To Diana,
Roses are red, violets are blue,
There's nothing in the world as
pretty as you.

RIGHT: Diana, fairy princess.

Diana
The CARING PRINCESS

One of the remarkable aspects of Diana's character was her caring nature. She developed great inner strength through her own adversities and found the ability to communicate through a look, a gesture or a touch. While listening to old people, children and those who were ill or felt rejected, Diana was able to give support and help them overcome many of their problems.

When the reports of her own illness and instability first came out, I didn't believe them. I thought she was doing her job, and doing it well. However, now that I know what she went through and how she climbed out of such a painful period, I am full of admiration for her.

RIGHT: Princess Diana was a caring princess.

Princess Diana was a caring princess. from LOLA
I love you Princess Diana and I wish you were still alive, lots of love Eleanor xxx
prince William and
very sorry your Mother
We feel your sympathy
was a great Mother to you and
princess were ever had and she
Be remeber as Queen of hearts
She touched sick people
and cared the world.
We will support
Through Tommor
From Laura aged 9

"Then I found myself being more and more involved with people who were rejected by society . . . and I found an affinity there. And I respected very much the honesty I found on that level with people I met, because in hospices, for instance where people are dying, they're much more real than other people and I appreciated that."

(Diana, November 1995)

"What makes these hidden addicts succeed in finding the confidence to take on real life again? A frequent reason is the support of their friends. If friends still stand by them they gain a greater sense of self worth, they begin to want to belong."

(Diana, November 1992)

RIGHT: *Dear Diana,*
Thank you for taking care of the sick people.
You were very kind. We were very sad when we
heard about the accident.
Your dresses were nice and you always
looked beautiful.
We feel very sorry for Prince William
and Prince Harry because they haven't
got a mum now.
You are still alive in our hearts.
Love Ryelands school

"Nothing can prepare you for the appalling pain and suffering anti-personnel mines can inflict on innocent children and civilians. It was so poignant, so very poignant. The little girl we met had had her intestines blown out. She was very, very poorly. I remember looking at her and thinking . . . what was going on inside her head and her heart . . . was very disturbing."

(Diana, January 1997)

"Every young person deserves a proper start in life and those who have no family to turn to need to be able to rely on us as a society for the help and encouragement they need. Everyone needs to be valued. Everyone has the potential to give something back if only they had a chance."

(Diana, December 1995)

RIGHT: *Thank you for being so good.*

Diana
As a MOTHER

Diana started work at a school for young children. Her interest, attention and patience were rewarded by love from her pupils. This experience with children, and the fact that she was fortunate to enjoy many happy times with both her parents, prepared her well for parenthood – a role she took very seriously.

She was just twenty when she married the Prince of Wales, and she had their two sons, William and Harry, within the space of three years. They now feel the loss of their mother dreadfully. She adored them and spent as much time as possible with them. She took them on demanding expeditions and participated in their activities. Diana wasn't afraid to get wet, swing her children or play silly games.

ABOVE: *Dear Diana,*
You were beautiful and we miss you.
Oliver and Ben
To William and Harry,
You had a lovely mum.

ABOVE: *Dear Prince William and Harry,*
I am sorry to hear about your mum.
I bet your mum is happy where she is. I bet that she will
think about you every day. I know you must be very sad.
Love from Sophie-Rose

LEFT: *God bless your children.*

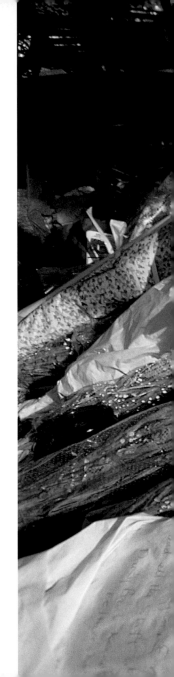

ABOVE: *Dear Princess Diana,*
I wish I could have cuddled you.
Love from Tom   Age 7

Diana
In HEAVEN

Diana's death shocked the world. It is sad that the protection insisted on by Prince Charles (even after the divorce) was not available when she was abroad.

As a Christian, Diana believed in life after death, and I'm certain she is now in heaven. Her father's death in 1992 upset Diana deeply, and she was quick to support others who lost loved ones.

I will always miss Diana. Her loss has left a terrible hole in our family, and her presence is irreplaceable. It is wonderful that so much of what she started and cared for is being continued.

The world is a much darker place without her, but the ray of hope we are left with is the memory of her warmth, her laughter, and her ability to care. We need to try and use these things which she left us in our own lives. This is her legacy.

*"As far as I know, crying has yet to kill someone.
It does not harm people to cry, or any bystanders. But there
seems to be a curious conspiracy in adults to suppress this
emotion . . . People keep trying to stop others from
crying as though it will harm them.
The hug is a simple and highly effective way of sharing
concern or showing approval. Like crying, a cuddle or hug
doesn't hurt. It is cheap, environmentally-friendly and needs
minimal instruction. Hugs can do great amounts of
good – especially for children."*

(Diana, November 1992)

"I'd like to be a queen of people's hearts, in people's hearts . . ."

(Diana, November 1995)

RIGHT: *We loved you, Princess Diana,
Hope you are happy in heaven with Dodi x x*

ABOVE: *R.I.P. Good night.*
RIGHT: *Diana with the angels.*